This story contain
high frequency w

mental

jammy dodger

cretin

Gwendoline

moist

Christmas 2022 was fast approaching and Tiff, Fish and Chipper's school had sent a letter home.

Mum and Dad had retrieved it, screwed up, in the bottom of Tiff's book bag. They had expected it to be asking about snacks for the Christmas party or some guff about the Carol service but it was something altogether different.

The government were in discussions to close the school due to lack of funding.

Parkview Primary School was on a fairly rough estate in northern England, full of bellowing chimneys and flat roofed pubs.

It's name was due to the park which it overlooked.

The park consisted of one swing, which was permanently thrown over the top rail by the older kids meaning the youngsters could never actually use it.

Despite the appearance of the area, the parents were very supportive of the school. And also the spell of home schooling over lockdown nearly sent them mental and they were keen to avoid a repeat of it at all costs.

They were aghast at the news and immediately set up a WhatsApp group. The group was called 'Save Parkview Primary from the inept government/what are you bringing to the Christmas party?"

Tracey

I'm going to set up a meeting with our MP to discuss the proposals. Pringles.

Kellie

To even consider this is outrageous. Mini quiche selection

Karen
This is unbelievable.
Jaffa Cakes.

Alina
I'll start making some
banners. Samosas

John
We should start an online
petiton straight away. I'll get
on it! Jimmy Dodgers.

John
petition LOL

Mandy
I'm fighting this all the way.
Do you remember the hell of
lockdown?! Um Bongo

Helen
This government are
complete plums. Plums

Sue
This is awful news! Those little pineapple and cheese stick things, you know the ones that look like a hedgehog?

John
Jammy LOL LOL

John
We should start an online petiton straight away. I'll get on it! Jimmy Dodgers.

John
Sorry, already sent that. LOL LOL LOL

Mandy
How do you remove people from a group?

The children sat on the floor with the news on the TV and immediately set about creating some posters which they attached to a stick so they could wave them.

"Make sure you check the spellings," said Mum, "It would kind of undermine the message that the school is doing a good job if there are mistakes on it."

"I've been thinking about this actually," said Dad.

"Oh yeh?" replied Mum, sarcastically.

"I mean, schools and the education system are just a form of mind control really aren't they? Maybe the kids would be better off being taught at home?"

"Hmm, so you're offering to do that then are you?" replied Mum.

Dad had just had a promotion at the pork pie factory where he worked. He was in charge of pumping the jelly in with a gun and he wasn't giving up that sweet gig for anyone.

"Couldn't you do it? I mean, I know that you've got the housework to do and everything but that must only take you, what, half an hour a day?" said Dad.

Mum glared at Dad with such ferocity that she looked as though she was about to combust.

"Good point, well made!" said Dad.

"Make sure that they're as neat as possible!" said Dad. "And no colouring out of the lines!"

"What's guvment?" asked Chipper.
"Don't get Dad started on that," said Mum,
"We'll be here for hours!"

Chipper had heard his dad talk about the
'guvment' before but he didn't understand
most of what was said. He was pretty sure
that a lot of it was swear words though.

"The government run the country,
Chipper. They decide all of the rules on
taxes and things like that."

what chipper thought
his dad was talking
about when he said taxes
↓

"Sounds boring," said Chipper.

Dad then launched into an impassioned speech about what the government should be doing. He talked for a solid 15 minutes and when he finally ran out of steam he asked Chipper if he had any questions.

"Can I go and play football now?" he asked.

The next day at school all of the talk was about the school closing. The children had pretty much all agreed that the school closing would be the best thing that had ever happened in their whole lives.

"Think about it," said Fish, "It will be like a snow day, EVERY DAY! We could do whatever we wanted - you could play on your Playstation or make TikTok videos or anything."

But then Chipper reminded everyone about Lockdown and how it wasn't all consoles and lounging around - they had to actually do some work.

Some of the children nodded in agreement and then one of the older boys said, "We have a right to an education.

If we just spend all day, every day playing then we won't be able to pass our exams and we'll all have to work at McDonald's."

"Good point, that wouldn't work at all, there are hundreds of us at this school, we couldn't all work at McDonald's. I mean, I know that our local one has capacity for 175 customers and a drive thru but even at peak time they only have 18 members of staff on shift," said Tiff, who had an unusual interest in the employment logistics at her local fast food outlet.

"So I guess we're going to have to fight the decision then," the children agreed.

"What can we do? Any ideas?"

"We could glue ourselves to our desks like those extinction rebellion lads?" suggested one pupil.

"Yeh, not a bad idea. We'd need to get some good glue though, the glue sticks that we use here are absolutely crud. They don't even stick paper to paper."

Their thoughts were interrupted by the school bell, it was lesson time.

It was the children's favourite lesson - cookery with Mrs Bakewell. The children found it endlessly funny that their cookery teacher was called Bakewell.

However, her name was a misnomer - she did not bake well. She actually couldn't cook at all.

Mr Bakewell would vouch for this. He often didn't actually know what he was eating - it could've been chicken pie, fish pie or apple pie, he was never sure and dare not ask.

Instead he would pay compliments such as: "Hmmm, this is delicious!" and "This has got a very interesting texture." He did this to protect his wife's feelings because he was sensitive like that.

And so he didn't have to cook himself.

Today's cooking recipe was a Vegetable Medley. This was greeted with groans from the children who despised vegetables.

"Can't we cook something proper for a change?" asked Tiff.

"When you say 'proper' what do you mean?" Mrs Bakewell replied.

"Something like Chicken Twizzlers?" suggested Tiff.

"CHICKEN TWIZZLERS? They are not proper food. I tell you what, if you can show me on this picture where the twizzlers are on a chicken then we'll cook them next time."

Tiff studied the picture and said, "The twizzlers are right here, next to the nuggets."

Talk of the school closure was a source of stress in the household, which came to a head when Dad left the toilet seat up AGAIN and didn't replace the toilet roll.

Dad decided to go for a long walk in the woods with the family pet, a Golden Retriever called Fluffy. Fluffy was possibly the stupidest animal to have ever lived and had the same IQ as a piece of wet cardboard. He only ever listened to you if there were sausages involved. If you weren't offering him a sausage then you were irrelevant to him.

Before they entered the woods, Dad spoke to Fluffy -

"Right Fluffy, listen up, DO NOT under any circumstances jump in any muddy puddles. If you do then there will be no more sausages for you. Ever!

This is what Fluffy heard -

BLAH FLUFFY, BLAH, BLAH BLAH JUMP IN ANY MUDDY PUDDLES. BLAH BLAH BLAH BLAH BLAH = SAUSAGES BLAH BLAH BLAH.

It was Dad's fault really. He had put Fluffy's lead down so that he could check some betting odds on his phone.

Fluffy saw a squirrel go darting between two trees and he immediately made a bid for freedom. Dad called after him but it was no use. Despite the fact that Fluffy had never caught a squirrel in his life and wouldn't know what to do if he did ever catch one he still gave chase.

FLuFFy ———>

The odds were heavily stacked against him - even more so than the pointless bet Dad had just placed on Rovers to win 7 corners before half time. All the squirrel had to do was scale a tree to the height of 2 metres and Fluffy was flummoxed. Even a particularly stupid squirrel could outwit the poor hound.

Dad lost sight of Fluffy so had to walk around the woods calling him. The children had chosen the name Fluffy and he had almost immediately regretted giving them naming rights.

 He would have much preferred something butch sounding like Tyson or, erm, Butch. But of course, the children got their way and now it was him walking around in public shouting,

"FLUFFY, WHERE ARE YOU?"

like an absolute Gwendoline.

When Fluffy eventually came bounding back around the corner every inch of him was covered in a sticky brown mud. He looked like he'd been involved in an oil spill accident.

As he drew nearer the reason for him returning to Dad became clear - he was being chased by a squirrel.

"OMG FLUFFY! You absolute cretin. It's going to take hours getting that off," screamed Dad.

Dad crept in through the back door and silently carried Fluffy upstairs and placed him in the bath. He doused him in some shampoo and then rubbed him down in a towel, which quickly turned from pink to brown. He hid the towel in the bottom of the wash basket and headed downstairs.

"Right, I'm off for a nice relaxing, candle lit bath," said Mum, "Nobody disturb me for at least an hour, maybe two!"

Dad winced but said nothing.

Approximately 12 seconds later there was a loud shriek and some swear words that would've made a sailor blush. They would've probably been heard down the end of the street as Mum discovered the tide mark around the bath and the dog hairs everywhere.

Dad suddenly remembered something very important that he had to do in the garage, with the door locked.

The end result of the parent's WhatsApp group was that they decided to have a bake sale to raise funds the keep the school open.

It was a resounding success, lots of the mums, dads and children made all kinds of cakes: chocolate fudge, victoria sandwich, fairy cakes with fancy icing and lots more.

Mrs Bakewell made a Banoffee pie which also sold out even though nobody knew what it was. She'd run out of condensed milk so had improvised with a bottle of PVA glue she found in the art cupboard. She saved a piece for Mr Bakewell who described it as 'lovely and moist but just a tiny bit claggy and hard to swallow'.

The sale raised a total of £124.60, which the parents thought was a fine amount but in actual fact would only pay the school's gas and electric bill for half a day.

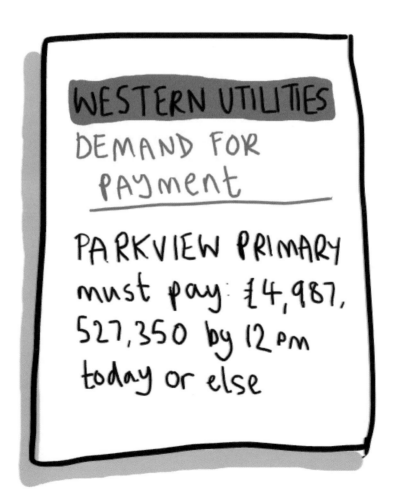

WESTERN UTILITIES

DEMAND FOR
PAYMENT

PARKVIEW PRIMARY
must pay £4,987,527,350 by 12 pm today or else

Over the course of the next few weeks, talk of the school closing died down. One morning Dad was reading his copy of the Daily Waffle and he noticed the headline - Education Secretary sacked!"

In his place a new secretary had been appointed and she had her own stupid ideas to implement so the plans to close Parkview Primary were shelved indefinitely! The school was saved!

The decision meant that the parent's current level of sanity would be protected. Everyone had a party to celebrate and a few people made a spectacle of themselves and became the subject of a new WhatsApp group.

Three cheers for Parkview!

Now, test your knowledge

Check your understanding:

1. When making the Banoffee Pie for the fundraiser, what did Mrs Bakewell use instead of condensed milk?

A) PVA glue   B) Arsenic   C)Sausages

2. Dad wanted to name Fluffy after a famous boxer, what was his name?

A) McGuigan   B) Calzaghe   C)Tyson

3. What did Dad compare Fluffy's IQ to?

**A) A lettuce   B) A piece of wet cardboard
C) A local radio DJ**

4. Mr Bakewell thought some of his wife's cooking was slightly unpalatable. How do you spell 'unpalatable'?
A) unpalatable
B) unpallitubul
C) yuk

5. One of the parents baked a chocolate fudge cake. How long, and at what temperature, should you cook one for?

A) 30 minutes at 180 degrees (fan assisted)
B) 25 minutes at 185 degrees (fan assisted)
C) 20 minutes at 190 degrees (fan assisted)

Answers:

1.A
2.C
3.B
4.A
5. It depends on your oven, consult your manual.

WIN WIN WIN!

If you enjoyed this book then please consider leaving a review on Amazon.
Doing so will automatically enter you into a competition to win a year's supply of chicken beaks.

Printed in Great Britain
by Amazon

23034218R00018